Contents

Text © Helen Hadley 1997
Illustrations by Andrew Keylock © STP 1997

The right of Helen Hadley to be identified as author of this work has been asserted by her in accordance with the Copyright, Designs and Patents Act 1988. All rights reserved. No part of this publication may be reproduced or transmitted in any form or by any means, electronic or mechanical, including photocopy, recording or any information storage and retrieval system, without permission in writing from the publisher or under licence from the Copyright Licensing Agency Limited. Further details of such licences (for reprographic reproduction) may be obtained from the Copyright Licensing Agency Limited of 90 Tottenham Court Road, London W1P 9HE.

First published by
Stanley Thornes Publishers Ltd
Ellenborough House
Wellington Street
Cheltenham
GL50 1YW

97 98 99 00 01 \ 10 9 8 7 6 5 4 3 2 1

A catalogue record for this book is available from the British Library

ISBN 0–7487–3379–5

Printed and bound in Great Britain

Introduction

Read, Write and Spell is a simple two book course which will teach your child to read, write and spell through sounds.

Read, Write and Spell workbooks are designed to help children develop early reading and writing skills and build a basic reading vocabulary. They learn to recognise letters, write them correctly and learn their sounds. They practise blending letters together to make words and using those words in reading, writing and spelling.

In order to do this your child will begin by using the sounds of letters as we say them in words rather than in the names we give them. For example do not use the long 'ay' sound when you say the name of letter 'a', use the short sound that you hear in 'at'. Use the sound of 'e' as it is said in 'end', 'i' as in 'it', 'o' as in 'on' and 'u' as in 'up' and so on. The more complex vowel and consonant sounds are left until Book 2.

The book is divided into sections. First, your child will learn the vowel sounds because every word they read or write uses one of the five vowels, a, e, i, o, u, or letter 'y'. Next come the sounds of consonants according to the place in the mouth where these letters are formed. This also helps your child to listen carefully to and identify letters whose sounds are similar. Try them out for yourself using the sounds of the letters. The groups are as follows:

tip of the tongue sounds	d	l	n	r	s	t
lip sounds	b	f	m	p	v	w
back of the tongue sounds	c	g	h	k	y
front of the mouth sounds	j	q	x	z

Once your child has learned the alphabet he or she will go on to learn these useful letter sounds: 'sh', 'th' and 'ch'. These letters are not called blends, because when put together they make a very different sound from the sound made by the individual letters. In the last section your child will practise building words with letters which form a blend at the beginning of a word.

The activities on each page will allow your child to practise the letter sounds he or she has learnt, and help to develop skills to decipher unknown words. Between each section there are three Review pages. These pages help you to check that your child has learned the letters in the previous section, and can remember them and use them in reading and writing.

Working at home

- Set aside some time each day for learning activities with your child at home. If your child has started school, given them time to unwind after returning home before you start work. Let them have a drink, a biscuit, a play, time to relax before you start.
- There will be days when your child does not feel like working; try to coax, but don't make a big scene. Accept it – there is always tomorrow.
- Choose a quiet time or place where there is no T.V., radio or other noise to disturb their concentration.
- Make sure that your child is clear about the task or activity and what it asks them to do.
- Talk with them about how they set about doing the activities. Getting them to talk with you now establishes communication patterns and a way of being together that pays dividends for the rest of your lives.

Here are some suggestions for working with your child at home on *Read, Write and Spell*:

- Work through no more than one page at a time.
- Spend two or three days working on activities and games related to that page.
- You will need to do some activities together so that you keep a check on what your child is doing, for example, learning to write a new letter shape. However, the directions are clear and consistent and your child will be able to read them and work through most of the other activities independently.
- Talk about each activity, work through it together, then leave your child to complete it before going on to the next one. Once the activities on a page have been completed reinforce your child's learning by going back through the page together asking how he or she did each activity and checking the answers.
- Praise your child's efforts in each activity. Be specific and tell them exactly what they have done well, so that they will know how to do well next time. Say things like 'I like the way you remembered which way round to write the letter,' or, 'You listened carefully to hear that sound in the middle. Well done,' or 'Haven't you found a lot of words for this letter. Where did you find them?'
- Try to keep to the page order, if you can, because the activities are built around the letters learnt earlier in the book.

- Every day play some of the letter and word games suggested below — and any others you can think of! Do spend some time each day on the games for the 'useful words' too, which are introduced on Review page 3. Because they make up one third of all reading and writing it is essential that your child can recognise these useful words on sight. This is why they are often referred to as 'sight words'.

Working with letter sounds

- **On the first day** work through the page. First of all look at the page. Ask: 'What do you think we are going to find out today? Do you know this letter? Have you seen it before?'

  Activity 1 Children first trace the large letter shape with the index finger of their writing hand saying the letter's sound as they do so. Each letter starts with an arrow leading from a dot, follows the arrows and ends at the cross. Trace the letter in a continuous movement several times using the index finger, pencil, crayons or felt pens. Once the movement has been mastered children should write over the dotted letters underneath using the correct movement then write the letter themselves between the lines. You should watch your child doing this to ensure that the movement is correctly formed.

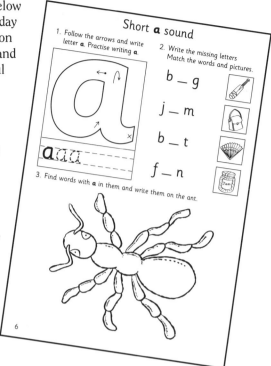

  Activity 2 In the vowel section children write the letter they are learning on the space in the middle of each word, say the word it makes and link it to the correct picture. In the following sections they say what is in the picture and write the missing letters. These missing letters will be the new letter being learnt plus others already learnt.

  Activity 3 Your child should look in books, newspapers, magazines, road signs, food packages, in fact anything with writing in it, or on it, for words with the new letter in them.

- **On the second day** go through the page again talking about the activities and finding more words.

- **On the third day** ask your child to think of more words with the letter sound in them, practise writing the letter and play some of the games suggested below.

Review pages

- **Review 1** focuses on letter recognition.

  Activity 1 asks your child to say what is in the picture and write the first letter underneath.

  Activity 2 requires children to say what is in the picture, point to the letter and say its sound then circle the letters in the right-hand box which are the same.

- **Review 2** focuses on spelling, listening for sounds and writing them down. First your child should say what is in the picture then write the missing letter(s) in the spaces underneath.

- **Review 3** covers reading, writing, spelling and useful words to be learnt.

  Activity 1 Your child should link the letters and pictures at the beginning but soon move on to filling in the name of what is in the picture from letters they have learnt. Printed words will be those they can build themselves or 'useful words' already learnt on previous Review pages. Once the missing letters have been filled in your child should read what is under the pictures.

  Activity 2 is a short story or sentences to read which use only words which your child can build or 'useful words' they have learnt.

  Activity 3 first asks your child to look closely at words. Later they start building and writing phrases and short sentences.

  Activity 4 lists six useful words for your child to learn. Some of these can be blended to make words but most of them have to be learnt as whole words. By the time children have finished this book they will have learnt forty such words. These forty words make up one-third of the words we use in all reading and writing – whatever our age.

The last page has a list of the 'useful words' learnt in this book. Place a piece of paper over all but the first row. Ask your child to look at the words in the first row, look at the pattern of the word's shape, look at the tall letters, the short letters, those with tails, then cover them and try to write them from memory in the boxes underneath. If children have trouble in remembering any let them have another peep. Only do two rows at a time. You do not have to wait until the book is completed to start work on this page. You may prefer your child to write the words from memory on a spare piece of paper so that you can play this memory game more than once. You can also dictate words at random from those your child has already learnt.

Games

Listening games

- Say three words beginning with the same sound, e.g. 'cut, cat, castle'. Ask your child which sound they hear at the beginning of each word. Ask for another word beginning with the same sound.
- Say four words, three of which begin with the same sound and the fourth with a different sound, e.g. 'dog, cat, dormouse, deer'. Ask which words have the same sound — what sound is it? Which one begins with a different sound — what sound is that?
- Play 'I spy with my little eye something beginning with the same sound as _____ (e.g. wall)'. Choose a word beginning with the same sound your child is learning or a letter sound already learnt.

Card games

- First of all cut a number of cards all the same size, from the backs of old Christmas or birthday cards. Make one set for the letters learnt and another for the 'useful words' being learnt. Make two cards for each letter or word. Add to your letter and word packs each new one as it is learnt. Write 1L on the back of the letters cards and 1W on the back of the word cards, or dab each set with different coloured paints. It speeds up sorting the packs after use.
- Put out cards for the letters already learnt. Place them face down. Ask your child to turn over a card and say the sound of the letter, and then give you a word beginning with that sound.

- Place the vowel cards face up and the consonant cards face down. Your child picks up two consonant cards, turns them over, then chooses one of the vowels which will go between the letters to make a word. If this is not possible they put back one of the consonants and turn over another.
- Put two copies of each letter or word card face down on the table. You and your child take it in turns to turn over two cards, saying what is on each card. If they match they are kept as a 'trick', but if they do not match they are returned, face down, to *exactly* the same place on the table. By remembering where cards are placed it is possible to find matching cards and win more 'tricks'.
- Place the word cards face up. Your child can put those together which begin with the same letter, end with the same letter or have the same letter in them, whichever you choose to do for that game.
- Place the word cards face up. Your child picks up one card, finds its matching pair and says the word.
- Hold the pack of word cards and as you turn them face up one by one your child reads the card aloud before you cover it with the next one. Play the game slowly at first but gradually turn the cards faster and faster.
- When your child is confident play the above game by the clock. How quickly can he/she go through the pack? How many cards can he/she read in one minute? And so on.
- Using the letter cards turn them over for your child to say the sound before the next one covers it.
- Play the above game but your child has not only to say the letter's sound but also a word that begins with that letter before the next is turned. Start with only ten cards and gradually build up as your child progresses through the book.

Short **a** sound

1. Follow the arrows and write letter **a**. Practise writing **a**.

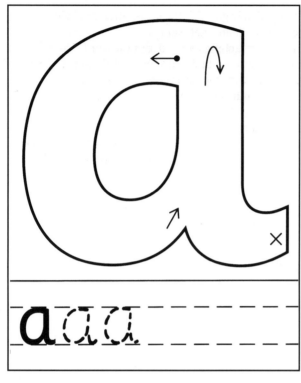

2. Write in the missing letters. Match the words and pictures.

b _ g

j _ m

b _ t

f _ n

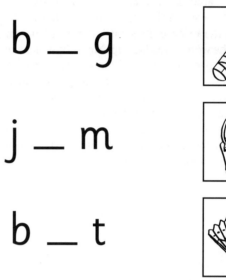
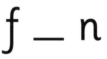

3. Find words with **a** in them and write them on the ant.

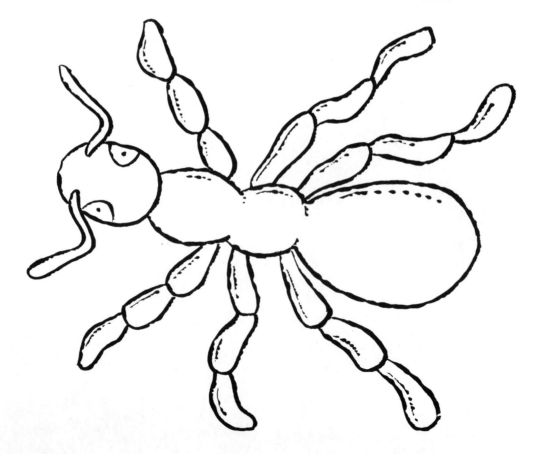

Short **e** sound

1. Follow the arrows and write letter **e**. Practise writing **e**.

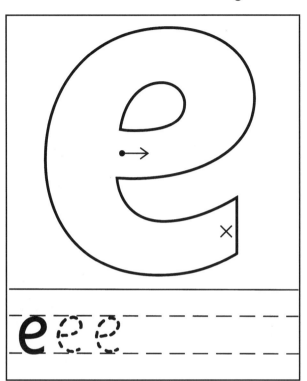

e e e

2. Write in the missing letters Match the words and pictures.

h _ n

w _ b

n _ t

l _ g

3. Find words with **e** in them and write them on the elephant.

Short **i** sound

1. Follow the arrows and write letter **i**. Practise writing **i**.

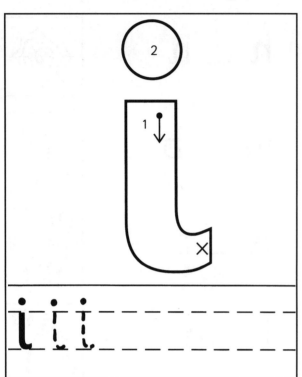

2. Write in the missing letters Match the words and pictures.

p _ n

z _ p

p _ g

l _ d

3. Find words with **i** in them and write them on the ink.

Short **o** sound

1. Follow the arrows and write letter **o**. Practise writing **o**.

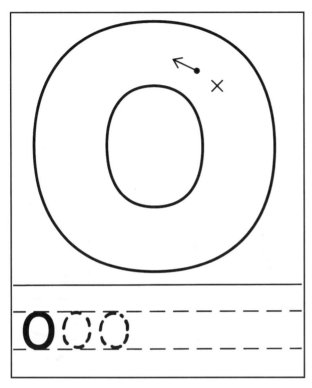

2. Write in the missing letters. Match the words and pictures.

p _ t

b _ x

d _ g

c _ t

3. Find words with **o** in them and write them on the orange.

Short **u** sound

1. Follow the arrows and write letter **u**. Practise writing **u**.

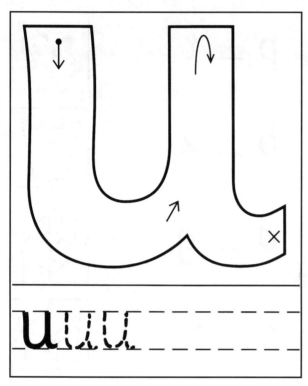

2. Write in the missing letters
   Match the words and pictures.

t _ b

c _ p

g _ n

s _ n

3. Find words with **u** in them and write them on the umbrella.

Review 1

1. Write the vowel for each picture.

2. Put a ring round the vowels that match.

(orange)	a	b c a o a a g
(egg)	e	o e c e a o e
(indian)	i	i j i l j i l j i
(orange)	o	o a o c e o c
(umbrella)	u	u n u v n m u

Review 2

Say what is in each picture then write the missing letters.

c _ n	d _ g	c _ t	w _ b
b _ n	c _ p	p _ n	l _ g
s _ x	n _ t	b _ n	h _ t
b _ s	v _ n	z _ p	n _ t

Review 3

1. Look at each picture. Say its name. Draw a line to the letter that is its middle sound.

a

e

i

o

u

2. Look at the word in the first box. Say its name. Circle the words in the second box that have the same middle sound.

bag	jam	web	ring	bat
hen	dog	net	bed	hat
pig	zip	led	pan	gun
box	fix	dig	pot	log
tub	pup	fan	sun	cap

3. Learn these useful words.

a	and	I	my	am	the

d sound

1. Follow the arrows and write letter **d**. Practise writing **d**.

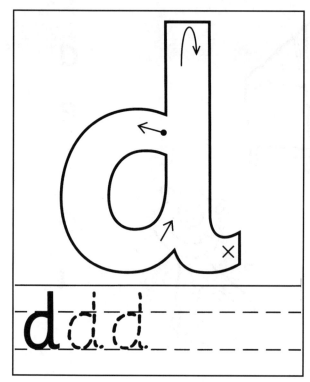

2. Write in the missing letters.

_ r u m

_ _ g

_ _ t

l _ _

3. Find words with **d** in them and write them on the dog.

l sound

1. Follow the arrows and write letter **l**. Practise writing **l**.

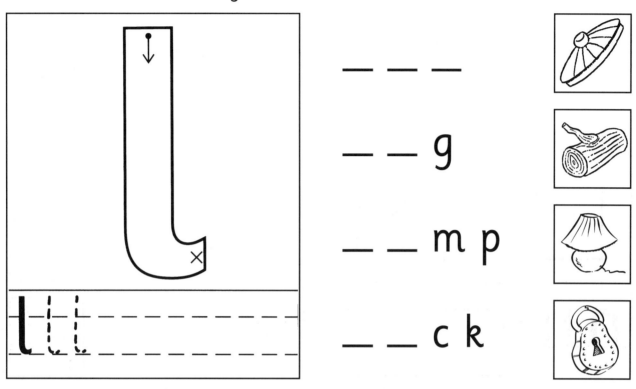

2. Write in the missing letters.

_ _ _

_ _ g

_ _ m p

_ _ c k

3. Find words with **l** in them and write them on the lolly.

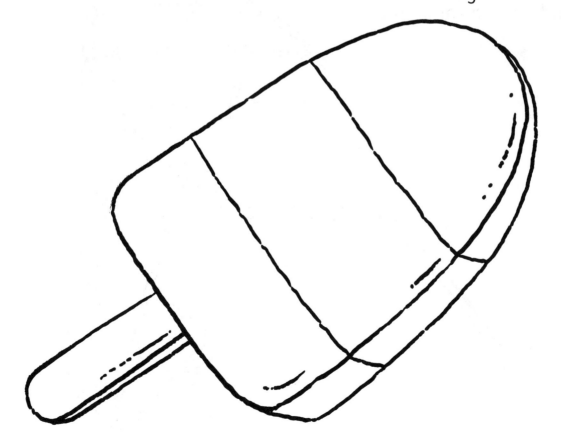

n sound

1. Follow the arrows and write letter **n**. Practise writing **n**.

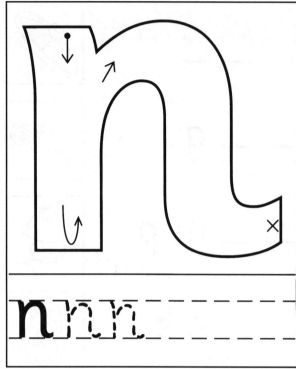

2. Write in the missing letters.

_ _ t

b _ _

_ _ t

p _ _

3. Find words with **n** in them and write them on the net.

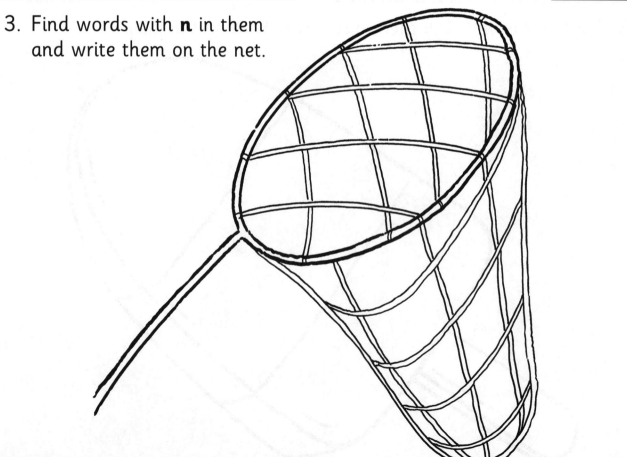

r sound

1. Follow the arrows and write letter **r**. Practise writing **r**.

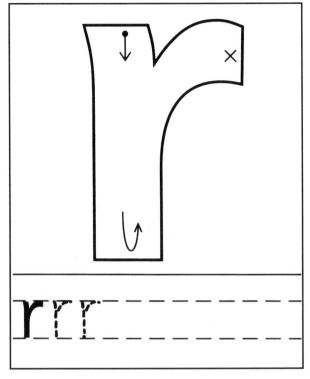

2. Write in the missing letters.

_ _ t

_ _ _

_ _ n g

f _ _ g

3. Find words with **r** in them and write them on the rabbit.

s sound

1. Follow the arrows and write letter **s**. Practise writing **s**.

2. Write in the missing letters.

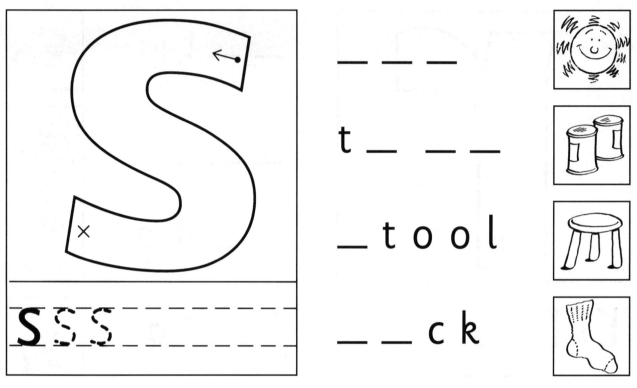

3. Find words with **s** in them and write them on the snake.

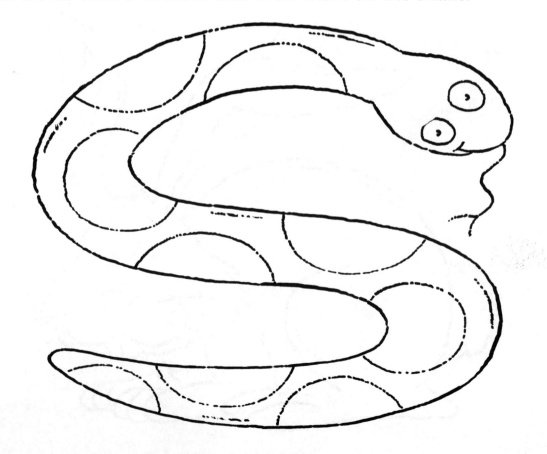

t sound

1. Follow the arrows and write letter **t**. Practise writing **t**.

2. Write in the missing letters.

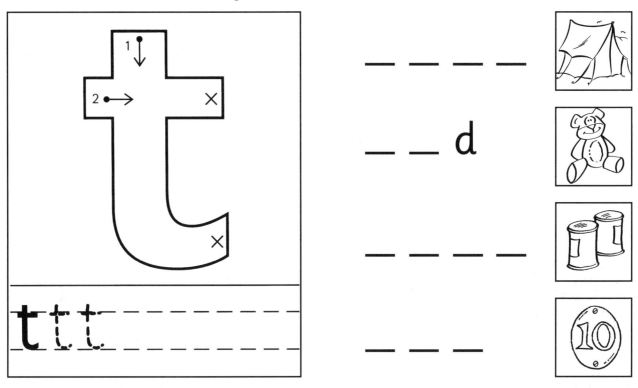

3. Find words with **t** in them and write them on the teddy.

Review 1

1. Write the letter for each picture.

2. Put a ring round the letter that match.

	d	d b h d k b d
	t	l t h k t l t
	r	n r m r i r n
	l	t l k h l l k
	n	m n u v n u n
	s	s z c s e s z

20

Review 2

Say what is in each picture then write its name.

_ _ _	_ _ _	_ _ _	_ _ _
_ _ _	_ _ d y	_ _ _	_ _ _
_ _ _	_ _ c k	_ _ g g	_ _ n g
_ _ b	_ _ g	_ _ p	b _ _ _

21

Review 3

1. Look at each picture. Say its name. Write it in the space under the picture. Read the words.

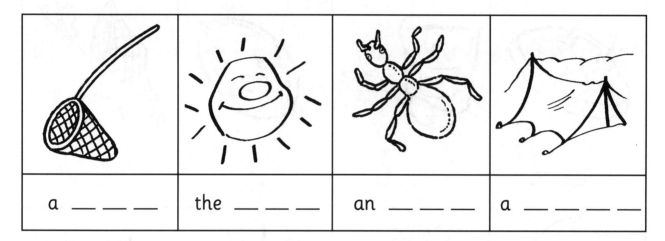

a _ _ _   the _ _ _   an _ _ _   a _ _ _ _

2. Read why the little girl is sad.

     I am sad.
                         I lost my doll.

     My doll is on the sand.

3. Choose one word from each and write the words on the line

a	log	_a log_	_the_
the	pan	_____	_____
my	rat	_____	_____
	ted	_____	_____

4. Learn these useful words.

it	is	in	at	to	of

22

b sound

1. Follow the arrows and write letter **b**. Practise writing **b**.

2. Write in the missing letters.

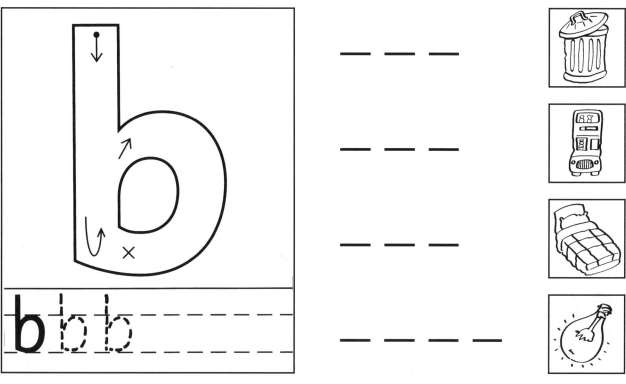

3. Find words with **b** in them and write them on the bee.

f sound

1. Follow the arrows and write letter **f**. Practise writing **f**.

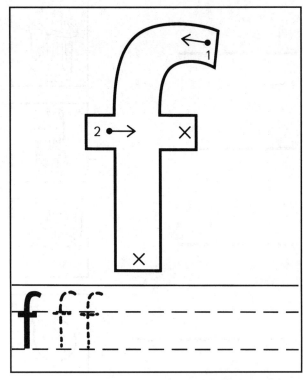

f f f

2. Write in the missing letters.

_ _ X

_ _ _

_ o o _

_ _ _

3. Find words with **f** in them and write them on the fish.

m sound

1. Follow the arrows and write letter **m**. Practise writing **m**.

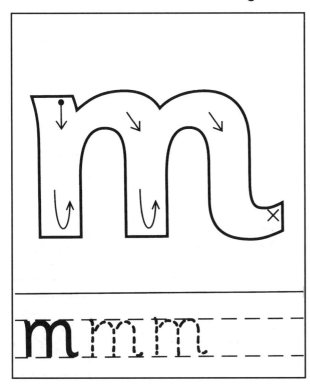

2. Write in the missing letters. Match the words and pictures.

_ _ _

_ _ _ k

h _ _

_ o o _

3. Find words with **m** in them and write them on the mouse.

25

p sound

1. Follow the arrows and write letter **p**. Practise writing **p**.

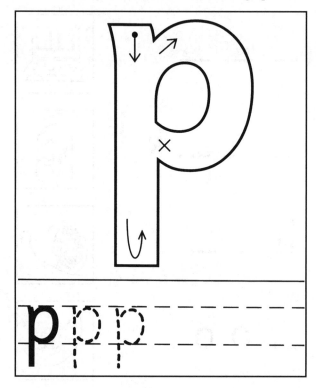

2. Write in the missing letters. Match the words and pictures.

_ _ _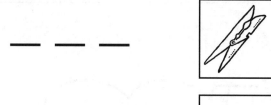

_ _ _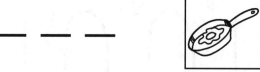

c _ _

c _ _

3. Find words with **p** in them and write them on the pig.

v sound

1. Follow the arrows and write letter **v**. Practise writing **v**.

2. Write in the missing letters.

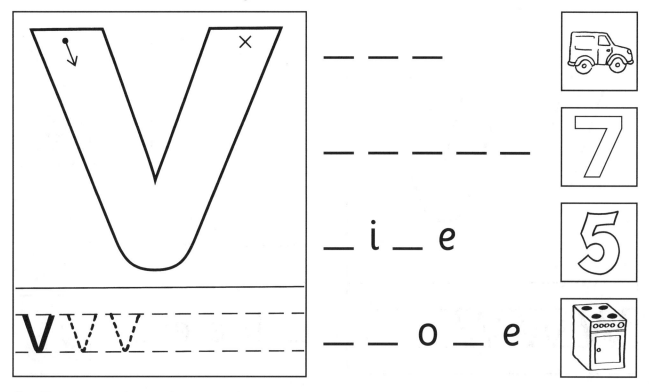

_ _ _

_ _ _ _ _

_ i _ e

_ _ o _ e

3. Find words with **v** in them and write them on the van.

w sound

1. Follow the arrows and write letter **w**. Practise writing **w**.

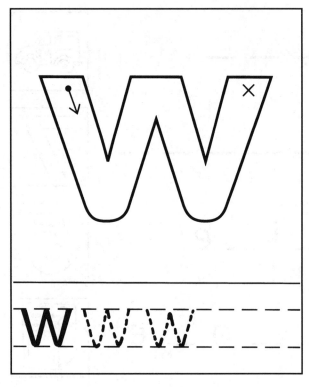

2. Write in the missing letters.

_ _ t c h

_ _ t c h

_ _ l l

_ h e e _

3. Find words with **w** in them and write them on the well.

Review 1

1. Write the letter for each picture.

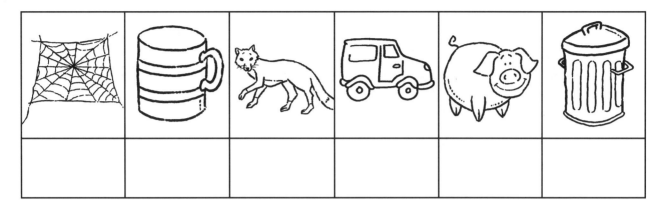

2. Put a ring round the letter that match.

m	n m w m w n w m
p	b p d q p q p d
b	d q b p b b q d
f	l f k b f b f k
w	m n w u w u m w
v	w v m v u v w m

Review 2

Say what is in each picture then write the missing letters.

_ _ _ _	_ _ _	_ _ _	_ _ _
_ _ _	_ _ _	_ _ _	_ _ _
_ _ _	_ _ _	_ _ _	_ _ _
_ _ _	_ _ _	_ _ _	_ _ _

Review 3

1. Look at each picture. Say its name. Write it in the spaces. Read the words.

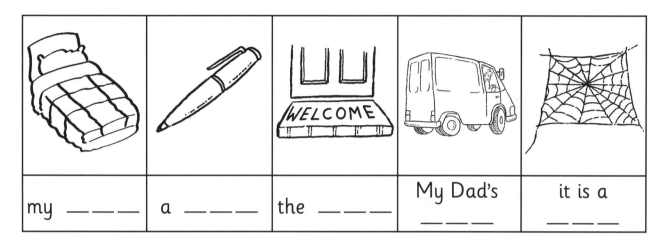

my _ _ _ _	a _ _ _ _	the _ _ _ _	My Dad's _ _ _ _	it is a _ _ _ _

2. Who is on my bed?

My Mum sits on my bed.   My teddy is on my bed.

My doll is on my bed.   I am in my bed.

3. Write about the pictures.

4. Learn these useful words.

that	then	this	he	was	said

31

c sound

1. Follow the arrows and write letter **c**. Practise writing **c**.

2. Write in the missing letters. Match the words and pictures.

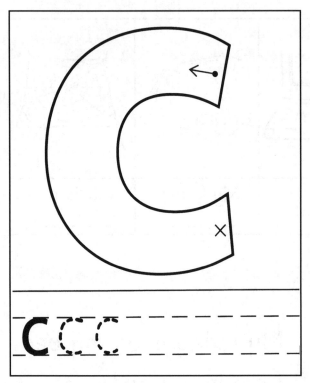

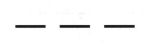

3. Find words with **c** in them and write them on the cat.

32

g sound

1. Follow the arrows and write letter **g**. Practise writing **g**.

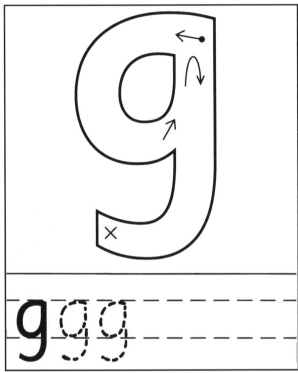

2. Write in the missing letters.

_ a _ e

_ _ _

_ _ _

_ _ _

3. Find words with **g** in them and write them on the gull.

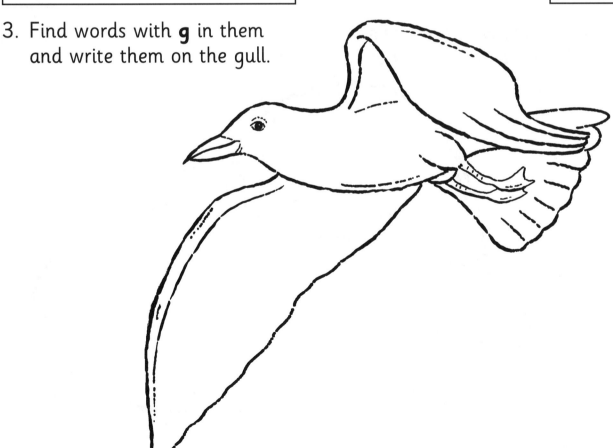

h sound

1. Follow the arrows and write letter **h**. Practise writing **h**.

2. Write in the missing letters.

3. Find words with **h** in them and write them on the hat.

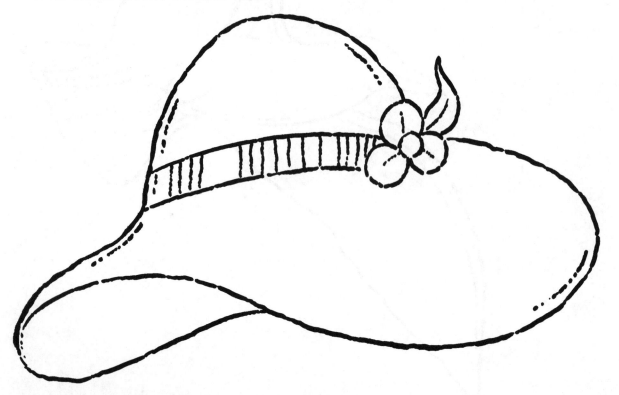

34

k sound

1. Follow the arrows and write letter **k**. Practise writing **k**.

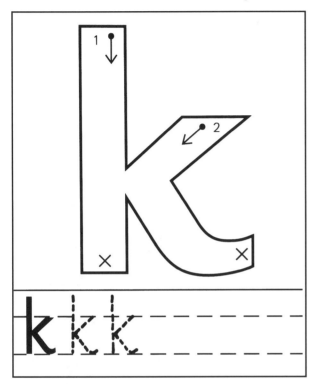

2. Write in the missing letters.

_ i _ e

_ _ _ k

_ _ n g

_ i _ e

3. Find words with **k** in them and write them on the kite.

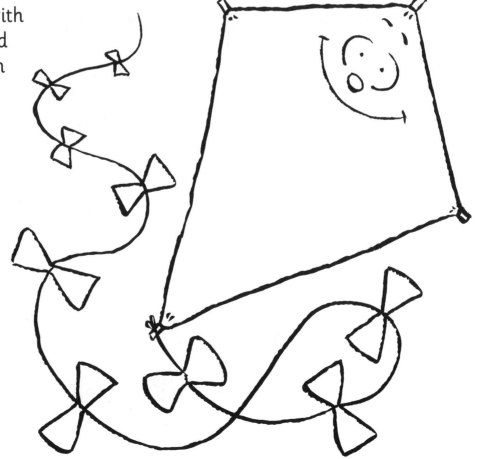

y sound

1. Follow the arrows and write letter **y**. Practise writing **y**.

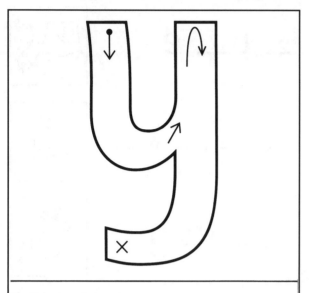

2. Write in the missing letters.

_ _ c h t

_ _ _

_ _ l k

3. Find words with **y** in them and write them on the yak.

Review 1

1. Write the letter for each picture.

2. Put a ring round the letters that match.

c	o c a c e a o c
k	l h k d k h k l
g	p g q y g p y g
h	k h b h d h k b
y	g y q p y g y p

Review 2

Say what is in each picture then write its name.

Review 3

1. Look at each picture. Say its name. Write it in the spaces. Read the words.

a _ _ _ _ of milk	my Mum's _ _ _	my _ _ _	my little _ _ _ _ _ e _

2. Who is on my bed?

My cat has six kittens.   My dog has seven spots.

My hen has ten   My 🐟 is in the tank

3. Write about the pictures.

4. Learn these useful words.

we	with	has	his	had	have

j sound

1. Follow the arrows and write letter **j**. Practise writing **j**.

2. Write in the missing letters.

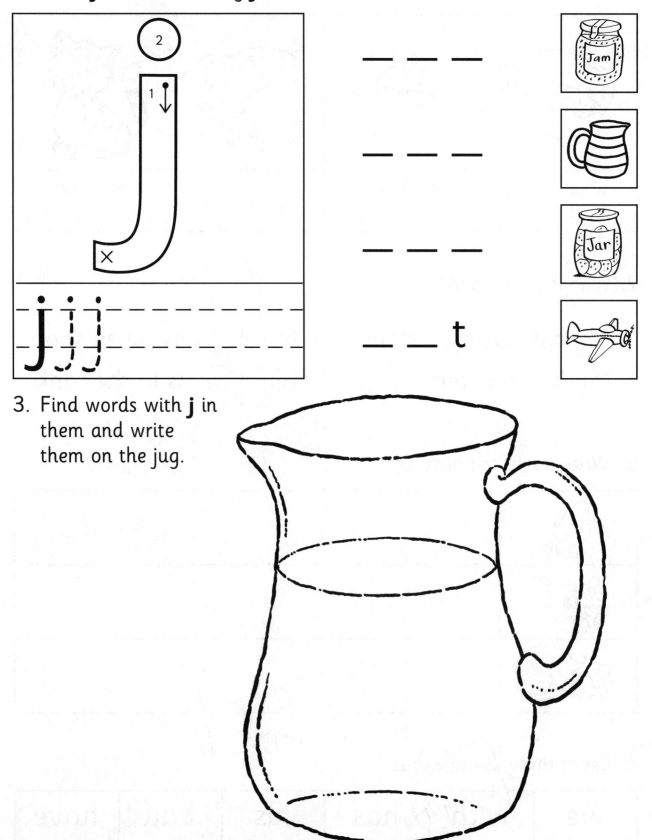

3. Find words with **j** in them and write them on the jug.

40

q sound

1. Follow the arrows and write letter **q**. Practise writing **q**.

2. Write in the missing letters.

_ _ e e _

_ _ _ _ l t

_ _ _ _ c k

3. Find words with **q** in them and write them on the quilt.

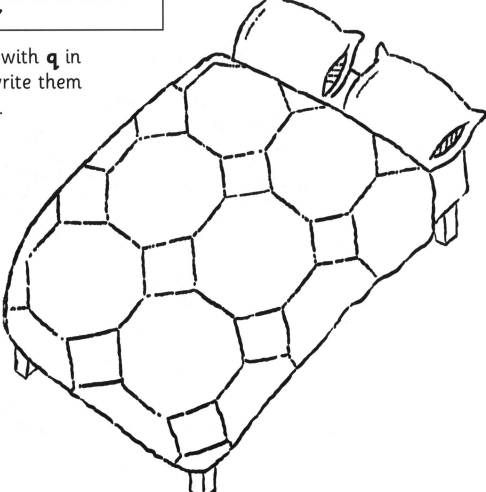

x sound

1. Follow the arrows and write letter **x**. Practise writing **x**.

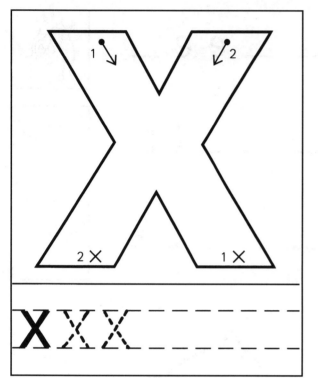

2. Write in the missing letters.

_ _ _

_ _

_ _

_ _ _ i

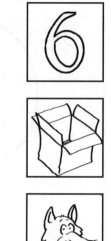

3. Find words with **x** in them and write them on the box.

z sound

1. Follow the arrows and write letter **z**. Practise writing **z**.

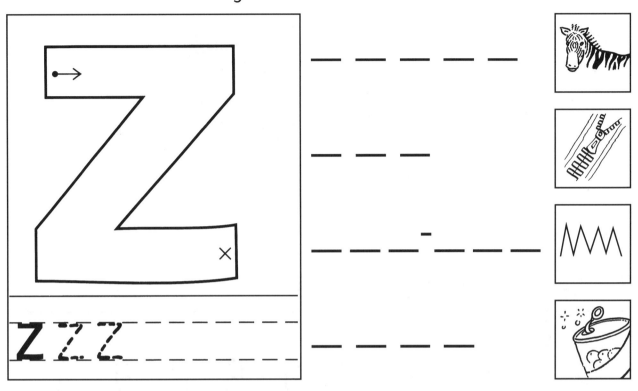

2. Write in the missing letters.

3. Find words with **z** in them and write them on the zebra.

Review 1

1. Write the vowel for each picture.

2. Put a ring round the vowels that match.

q	p q g q p g q
x	x z v x s x z
z	s z x z s s z
j	j l y j i y i j

3. Write six really useful words from memory.

Review 2

Say what is in each picture then write its name.

_ _ _	_ _ _	_ _ _	_ _ _
_ _ _	_ _ _	_ _ _	_ _ _
_ _ _	_ _ _	_ _ _	_ e e _
_ _ _ _	- _ a y	_ _ _	_ _ _ _

Review 3

1. Look at each picture. Say its name. Write it in the spaces. Read the words.

fill up the	we have a	this is a	I saw a

2. Read about Max, the fox and me.

I went to the hut. My pal max was in the hut. We saw a fox. It ran up the hill. Max ran up the hill. I ran with him but we lost the fox.

3. Write about the pictures.

4. Learn these useful words.

me	go	come	out	when	her

sh sound

1. Write in the **sh** sound to complete the words.

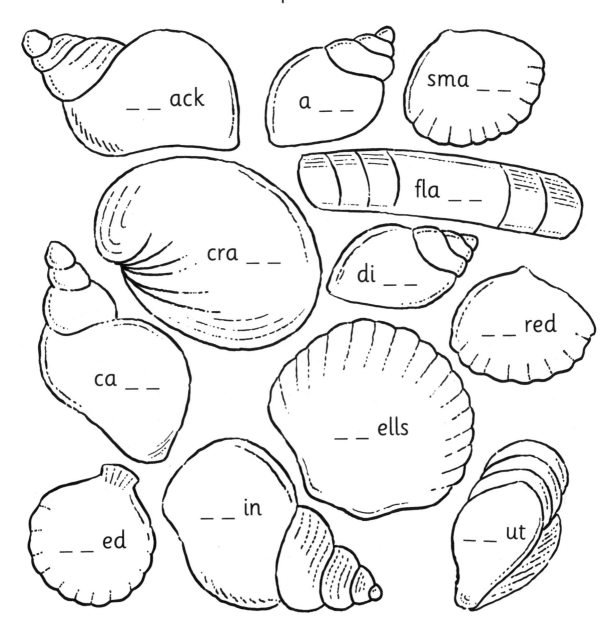

_ _ ack

a _ _

sma _ _ _

fla _ _

cra _ _ _

di _ _ _

_ _ red

ca _ _ _

_ _ ells

_ _ ed

_ _ in

_ _ ut

2. List the words you have made.

th sound

1. Write in the **th** sound to complete the words.

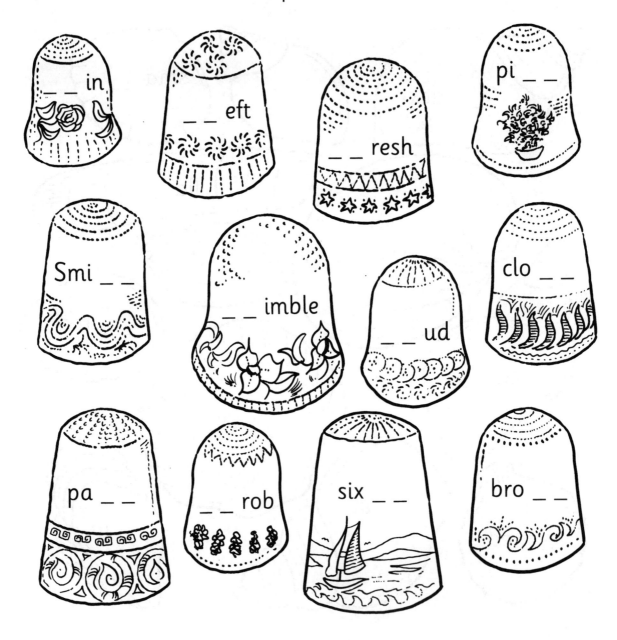

_ _ in

_ _ eft

_ _ resh

pi _ _ _

Smi _ _

_ _ imble

_ _ ud

clo _ _

pa _ _

_ _ rob

six _ _

bro _ _

2. List the words you have made.

th sound

1. Write in the **th** sound to complete the words.

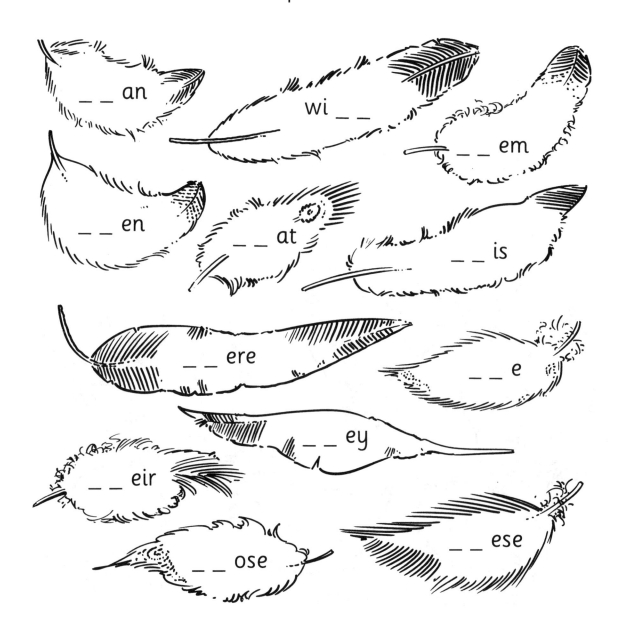

_ _ an

wi _ _

_ _ em

_ _ en

_ _ at

_ _ is

_ _ ere

_ _ e

_ _ ey

_ _ eir

_ _ ese

_ _ ose

2. List the words you have made.

ch sound

1. Write in the **ch** sound to complete the words.

fin _ _

mu _ _

crun _ _

ben _ _

_ _ ap

ri _ _ _

_ _ it

_ _ op

in _ _

_ _ ick

_ _ est

_ _ ill

2. List the words you have made.

Review 1

1. Write the missing letters for each picture.

_ _ u m b	_ _ e e p	_ _ u r _ _	s i x _ _	h u t _ _	r a _ _

2. Put a ring round the letter that match.

	sh-	shop chill shin chimp shut
	ch-	chip ship that chap chop
	th-	chat thud shod thin throb
	-sh	wish much mash pith cash
	-ch	sash bunch broth lunch munch
	-th	pith tenth inch path lash

3. Write six really useful words from memory.

Review 2

Say what is in each picture then write its name.

_ _ c k	_ _ _ _	_ _ ble	_ _ _ _
_ _ e e	_ _ or	_ _ air	_ _ _ _
_ _ ll	_ _ ee	_ _ ur	_ _ _ _
_ _ a i _	_ _ cken	_ _ _ _	_ _ a r

Review 3

1. Look at each picture. Say its name. Write it in the spaces. Read the words.

t __ __ __ is my doll	a big __ __ __ __	my Dad is __ __ irty	I can __ __ __ __

2. Read these sentences. Circle the best word to finish the sentence.

Josh went to the	ship shop chop	
Chad sat on the	lunch bunch bench	

3. Write about these pictures.

4. Learn these useful words.

she	there	they	see	here

bl, cl, fl, gl and sl sounds

1. Choose the right sound to make the words.
   Write it in the spaces.

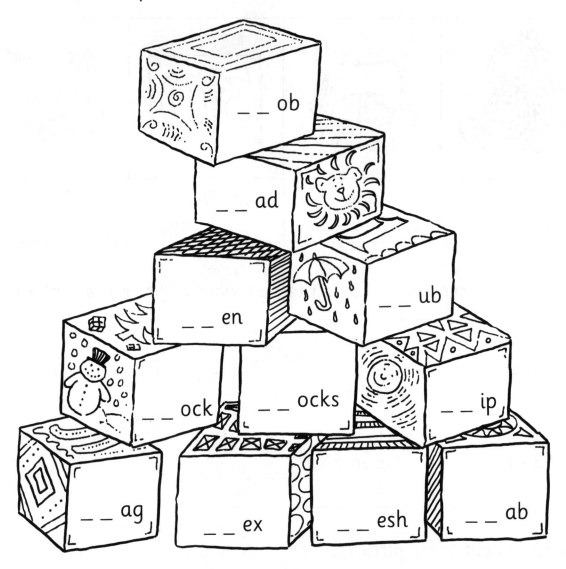

__ ob

__ ad

__ en

__ ub

__ ock

__ ocks

__ ip

__ ag

__ ex

__ esh

__ ab

2. List the words you have made for each sound.

54

br, cr, dr, fr and gr sounds

1. Choose the right sound to make the words.
   Write it in the spaces.

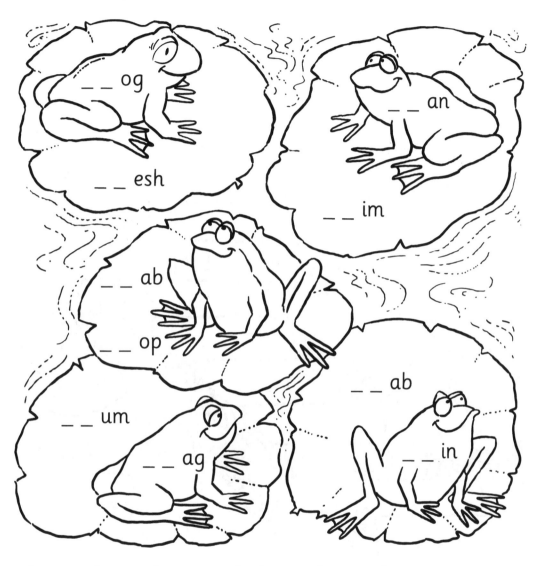

2. List the words you have made for each sound.

st sound

1. Write in the **st** sound to complete the words.

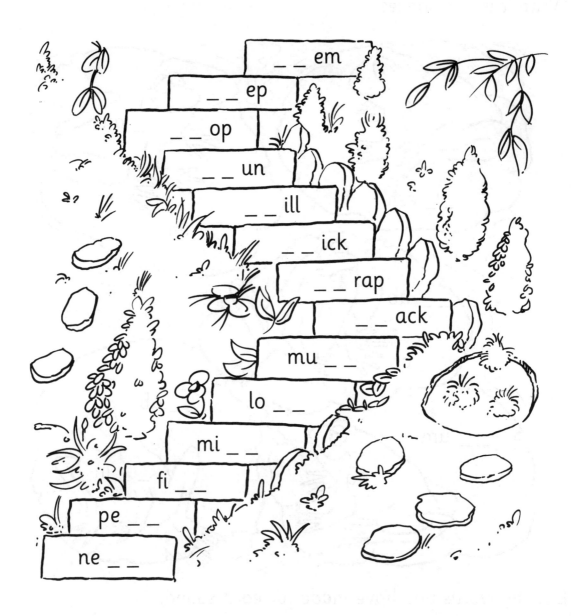

___ em

___ ep

___ op

___ un

___ ill

___ ick

___ rap

___ ack

mu ___

lo ___

mi ___

fi ___

pe ___

ne ___

2. List the words you have made.

sp sound

1. Write in the **sp** sound to complete the words.

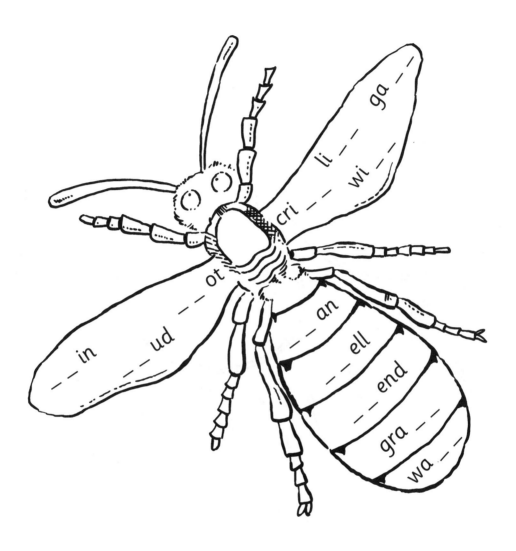

2. List the words you have made.

sk sound

1. Write in the **sk** sound to complete the words.

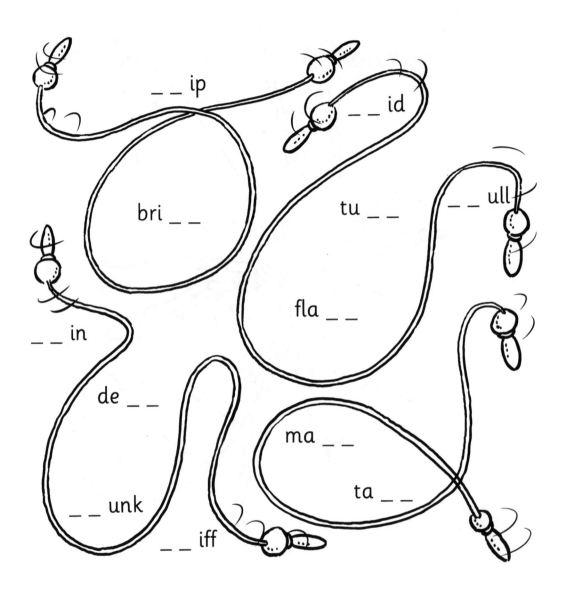

_ _ ip

_ _ id

bri _ _

tu _ _

_ _ ull

_ _ in

fla _ _

de _ _

ma _ _

ta _ _

_ _ unk

_ _ iff

2. List the words you have made.

sc, sm and **sn** sound

1. Choose the right sound to make the words.
   Write it in the spaces.

2. List the words you have made for each sound.

sw and **tw** sound

1. Choose the right sound to make the words.
   Write it in the spaces.

_ _ itch

_ _ enty

_ _ elve

_ _ ist

_ _ in   _ _ ig

_ _ an   _ _ ish

_ _ ift

_ _ amp

_ _ ept   _ _ ell

_ _ iss   _ _ im

2. List the words you have made for each sound.

Review 1

1. Write the first two letters for each picture.

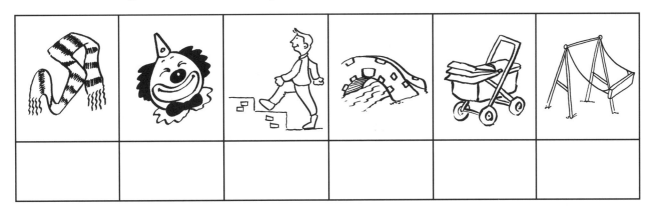

2. Cross out the non-words. Put a ring round the words that match. Write the real words in the box.

spill slip plis slip slup	
blue club culb clud club	
drap brop drop prod drop	
gorf frog forg grof frog	
brag grab barg grab garb	

3. Write six really useful words from memory.

Review 2

Say what is in each picture then write its name.

_ _ ou _ _	_ _ c k	_ _ _ _	_ _ a r
_ _ o w	_ _ a _ e	_ _ _ _	_ _ cker
_ _ e e	_ _ _ _	_ _ _ _	_ _ _ _
_ _ c k	_ _ _ _ sses	_ _ _ _	_ _ _ _

Review 3

1. Look at each picture. Say its name. Write it in the spaces. Read the words.

a __ __ own is funny	I can __ __ __ __	Mum fed the __ __ icks	we went on the __ __ ain

2. Read these sentences. Circle the best word to finish the sentence.

Ross	spelt swift swept	the	swing string spring
Stan went up the			stops straps steps

3. Write about these pictures.

4. Learn these useful words.

one	some	are	for	little

Check sheet

and	egg	it	on	up
dog	lip	net	ran	sun
ten	bin	fun	man	pet
van	wet	cut	gap	hen
kit	yes	jam	quit	box
zip	ship	chop	then	thin
blot	clip	flat	glad	plus
slot	splash	brim	crab	drum
frog	grab	pram	trim	stop
spin	skip	scan	smug	snap
swim	twig	brisk	lisp	lost